I0095258

NATURAL WONDERS

FINNS WAY BOOKS POETRY SERIES
Kate O'Keefe, Editor

NATURAL WONDERS

Patrick Stevens

FINNS WAY BOOKS

Published by Finns Way Books
Oakland, California

Copyright © Patrick Stevens
March 1, 2024
All rights reserved

Manufactured in the United State of America

ISBN 979-8-9899422-0-6

DEDICATION

For my father and mother who raised me to love nature and find joy in all of its gifts. I have spent my life enthusiastically searching out new sights and sounds in some woods or other. I have rarely been disappointed, always finding some new view or object or thought to move me onto another path. It is a wild life.

Patrick Stevens

Contents

Prologue

Winter

Spring

Summer

CONTENTS

AUTUMN

EPILOGUE

Old Growth

NATURAL WONDERS

Patrick Stevens

PROLOGUE

Raven

I woke up knowing
who we had been
before all the stars were placed
and oceans flowed free and new,
before our sun was firm in the sky,
the moon but in the making.

We were all called raven then
before men became men.
We were one
washing down mountain streams
spread to every shore.
We danced in the light
of a sun blue and bright,
just as we now come together
and dance in the moonlight,
the stars and the twinkle
together echo raven.

We were specters.
Shadows on the moon
winds made of sun.
We were the waves,
tides, the toll of time.
We glided through the sky
cresting high
always ever higher,
rising raven
Pure as light
thick as wind
pulsing the blood
of mother earth.

We colored this world
with rainbow wings
red, blue, yellow, white,
a universe blindingly bright.
Our wings spread sunshine
wherever we rose
wherever we lived
even here
under these dark firs
giving all the rainbow
to this world.
Swish, swishing high,
swooping whoop diving
warble coo
drop whirl thrust up
most colorful birds
flying high above this
cold spare world
spreading colors bright.

Or fluttered low,
Oh so low now
to feast through the night
to eat
to sleep
to warble
in deep piney woods
so dark away raven
now dark, hidden
we be raven.

GROUNDING

If each day
I can hear the wind rustle
through the trees,
feel a breeze brush my brow
as I step into the cool morning,
then all is well and right.

Or reach to touch the sun rising east,
moon setting west,
see endless, deep starry skies
pierced through and through
blue light, blue dark, blue darker.

I see no reason
to wish away this world,
strive for a better earth.
No more than that cardinal
chirping high,
a loon calling forlorn,
would I mourn the night,
regret a new day?

Each morn begins as best it can,
season in and season out.
Each with a new joy.
A bloom,
a new birthed chick,
snow piled thick and crisp.

It is my work
to find the wonder
and hold it close
for me to see.

WINTER

MOTHER AT REST

My forest is lonely
come January
when trees speak with
snowflakes and frost,
whispering a dialect easily lost
under crackling footfalls,
as we walk these trails
seeking to find her voice,
letting us know how she thrives
under earth
when all the world is
stark and bare.

I can hear my mother calling.
She says, "I will be fine.
We will awaken soon,
under warm spring breezes.
Resting, we are now here,
under warm, snow cover.
We dream softly,
as should you.
A little nap is our due."

She chuckles a bit
in her night,
laughing as we tip,
careful not to slip,
past an open spring brook
still gurgling
below thin ice,
tempting a taste.

No rustle of wind tossed leaves.

No herd of scampering squirrels,
nor the beat of does' hooves
bursting through the brush
nor the bleat of their babes.
No rush flutter of robins or thrush
rising scattered through the canopy,
chased from their worm work.
Those remembrances of spring.

Today,
just mother, whispering
bright, with a little laughter,
as we pass another brief,
long shadowed day,
walking in the sun.

First Winter Morning

Last night the breeze sculpted
new swooping snow bridges
thrust limb to limb,
a good inch deep
at least,
running across boughs
in that alder break
out back.

This will be my altar
where limb meets sky
today before sun rise
and full light
chickadees and juncos
flit though
to ground and up
feeding on small
sprouts and seeds
released by the wind
overnight.

It is a fine cathedral
for a smaller god,
one who hears
my whispered
"come here, come in,"
as I call my pups
back from the night,
quiet so as not to fright
the avian feast so near.

Magically a slit
moon's shadow drifts

crossing snow heaps,
a light breeze shifts
snow clumps loose
to pop and drop.
Soon the branches bare
will be better fare for birds
to perch on a bright day
well hid and safe.

Their sanctuary.
It is a fine cathedral
for a smaller god.

Survival

We winter well
here north
within our dark days,
short, ever shorter,
long cold nights,
so crisp the stars stand
upon us cold
as their lights flicker
sparkling the snow.
Quiet now,
the earth is closed,
huddled, nested,
waiting spring.

There lies a great poplar
toppled this past summer,
storm blasted,
root ball wrestled loose,
now sinking back to earth,
a great long pale
monster tree stretched out
along the forest floor,
becoming food
for mosses, lichen,
beetles, and birds
gathering now
to celebrate its demise.
Great colonies
within-without this new home
born of wind and gravity safe,
a metamorphic rest
feeding lives through to spring.

Tracks along the forest floor
reveal that others
live winter differently,
through these dark days.
That plump bear cub,
born a year past,
fattened on berries, fish,
acorns all summer long,
who I tracked down
a wooded October trail,
now hid beneath,
denned in a world of dreams
better for him
than winter's stark earth.

He saves his future
as winter goes,
in fantastic slumber
this season away,
deep beneath
sheltering snow,
carrying life
through to spring.

While we of the North
carry another year
past its last full moon,
its most short day,
its most long night,
and wait the rising
spring.

WINTER STORE

I see autumn closing down
as I pass the arbored vines
set south of my house.
An acrid odor,
dying, drying grapes
fills the air
since I did not harvest
fruits before first frost.

I had no need
to pluck and process
these sweet fruits,
for last season's jelly jars
still take space
on my cupboard shelves.

My hope is for
waxwings, black birds,
young bear and fox
who may visit at dusk,
or tomorrow,
to strip the grapes
clean the vines,
building their
winter store.

It is their due,
the debt I owe
for the delight I feel
watching them slip
through the forest
or drift with the wind.
Such wonderous sights,

living fine lives
I cannot even imagine.

Mother earth
holds us fair and just,
her endless riches
for all living creatures,
animals and man.
She gives me grace
to share what's given
free
from her to me.

Not every season's harvest
need be hid
and hoarded safe.
Leave a tithe for the rest,
or soon our world
would be stripped bare
where once all things natural thrived.

Taking Root

My geranium's
slipped stems
are hung,
suspended inside
Ball-Kerr glass jars,
in clear tepid water,
set along garage windowsill,
recreating the primogenitor
bathing in the sunrise
alive.

I see new tendrils
reach each morning
as they greet the day,
seeking life's magic,
their roots drift down
in rays spread
translucent through liquid,
wandering ever deep
in an amniotic underwater light,
like kelp in the ocean,
here on my shelves.

I dream the ocean's rhythm,
I see otters diving,
in amongst fronds cool and deep,
to retrieve succulent seashells
from the rocky bottom
so happy sweet.

It is morning
in the Midwest.
I love that life

replicates and thrives
most anywhere,
its bloom-bursting beauty,
even in a jar
in deep winter
on my garage shelf.

I can vision otters rising
and flowers blooming
the spring breeze
rise, rise, rising,
set free.

ICING IN

As sure as I sit here
on this summertime bench
watching the river freeze,
a breeze will blow
last autumn's leaves,
browned last gasps
of a season well past,
down to wash
into the ice
trapped through
to spring.

I feel January
folding in upon me,
narrowed nearly gone to ice,
this river froze below the bank.
I yearn clear water flowing free
sweeping the valley clean,
the smell of fresh, frost-heaved earth
broken by the heat of
a high hot sun,
the air beginning to bloom.

For now
the long shadow I cast
is wrapped in a winter white coat
all the burble hid
'til the rush of spring.
It is surely winter
dark and heavy
icing in.

I grow old in this frozen season
seeing my teachers
no longer stirring my imagination.
All those knowing sages,
stern task masters,
old as stone they seemed,
standing to align my eyes.
Sun, moon, and seasons
celestial navigators
warriors with cause
dragging my limp mind
awake each dawn,
or at the least
giving it a go.

Winter Roots

Through a rocky
highland morning
the oaks, maples, and ash
whisper *thank you*
to the cool winter wind—
now coursing through
their limbs as we
walk the forest floor—
for freeing them of their
leafy summer burden,
which wore them thin
though the past three seasons,
haunting their trunks,
giving refuge to ants
and mean mosses,
even on bright
summer days.

Leaves sucking
juices up and up
to hold the light
from darkened bark,
trading lush beauty
for a moment in the sun.
We see no shade now,
just shadow and white
shadow and light.

The trees are not asleep.
Now their roots dance
I hear them pop
on these silent cold days
in January.

Their deep energy holds,
awaiting warm spring rains
to unleash the dance
the sway of the sun
for another run
at summer.

WINTER WOOD

A good wood fire
holds through a night
once lit, always bright.
Old timers will tell you
wood heat's best,
as it warms twice,
once in the harvest,
once in the hearth.

I love the fragrant odors
of cedar and pine
blade sharp, tight wound
chain whir chipping
through their cores.
Fireplace long, ready to split
short sticks off each trunk,
kindling for hardwood fires,
maple, oak, and elm,
whose coals will hold
a house warm all night,
ash bed glowing
through to daylight.

Hard woods split
stacked separate to dry
in rows head high
under a tin-covered shed,
autumn air draws damp
from split wood
that we'll need
for first evening heat,
or to break frost
come some cold morning.

The old timers will tell you
wood heat's best
as it warms twice;
once in the harvest,
once in the hearth.
But I say it is the glow
under the ashes
that makes wood heat best,
giving us its warmth
through darkest times.
It holds like love
warming each of us
once kindled,
ever carried,
never to be lost.

SOLSTICE MIRACLE

It is near winter solstice
here on this cold earth
near the Moosehead River
where water still flows—
water will always move
deep through to spring.

Cool earth, warm air above
makes fog.
Night mists drape brown oak leaves,
buck brush twigs show a frosty rime.
Each morning I walk
to see what beauty might be left
in these dark, darker days.

Down at riverside,
a deer may cross my path
or I could flush a grouse,
and surely squirrels will skitter
in the trees as I pass,
crunching my way through to
an early spring.

Time, I know, is tick-tocking
to a sticky, thick summer day,
away from this cold old winter
that sneaked past October
to me here today.

I don't mind these
so short days
long light-lit nights.
I don't mind cold.

I don't mind slipping and sliding
all of my way
every day.

But just once, I'd like to see
this measure of night
magically burst,
not by carol or festive tree,
but by the chirrup
of a robin outside
on the lawn in sunrise,
pulling a fat worm
for breakfast on the day
of solstice eve.

Snow gnome

In January
after snowfall has paled
all the fallen leaves,
summer's green lawn
drifted alabaster,
the rose hedge,
marks a border line,
standing linen draped sentinel,
branches pulled low.
My yard this night white,
sparkling in moon glow,
a ghostly stage lighted,
awaiting the show.

So I awake
in a midnight world
locked near darkness
here, well past solstice
where all Christmas candles
have dimmed and gone.
New year's fireworks
burst and bombed,
away, away in the night
waiting day.

I stand watching east
under a dark mooned sky.
For this moment
light lies in the earth,
my world tipped topsy,
birch, poplars,
my small apple tree
stand on guard,

rising from light to dark;
from crystal earth,
into some dim end above
I cannot seem to see.

Here hidden shadowed,
I see no sun,
brightening winter's stark land
now ruled by vixen
and rabbits and owls,
on this cool crisp stage
where I rest unseen
waiting to witness
the dance.

I sense these sprites.
I see winter gnomes,
a frosty princess or two
pirouetting through
a shadow world.
I will join
their dance soon, too.
It is time, I think,
for frolic in the night.
or to bay at the moon.

The Soo Line Tracks

Footprints,
tracks
made deep each hour
where sun rays
do not cross
my snowy way
in passing.

Each belongs,
creature perfect,
impressed fresh,
just right made
like cookie cutter
hooves, paws, claws,
little bird feet
leaving their memories behind.

I walk today migrating
where the great Soo Line railroad
once hauled all the great trees
and rich iron ore off to market.
Where rolled nothing but money
for decades plus years.

The whoosh and roar
of those magnificent
old coal chug-a-chug engines
bursting my memory
as I see sign of small lives,
little mammals and birds,
now passing by here
in the quiet hush
of another snowy morning;

All the bustle clang-banging
rail cars gone;
even the iron rails ripped up,
melted,
ties turned to dust.

Just me following
the trail,
this worn passage,
leaving my footprints
with the rest
all strung along
the Soo-Line-
no-more.

SUGAR PLUM DREAMS

What do trees dream
in winter when
rest is all that matters?

Today my garden
became bare,
every last leaf
wind driven
off the little plum tree
planted last spring.

Through summer it thrived.
When the wind blew
It snap-danced pirouettes,
bent lithe, supple
green-bright in sunlight:
lime, khaki, verdant.
It waved a flag of youth.

Now, left a bare stick
facing the cold season,
snow, icy cold,
mice nibble its bark.
So comes winter,
the killing season.

Will its roots weave
mother-earth tales
of ancient forest groves,
where towering oaks ruled,
or talk of sweet orchard rows
where cousin apricot
and peach bloom

their fragrant lives?

I hope what dreams
my little plum weaves
bring a warm spring,
sweet blooms to brighten
my eyes as spring rains
waken a long winter sleep,
restoring the zest
for another summer dance.

Shadow

Always a dim light
hangs high above
my sky in any season,
night, day, twilight,
moon set or rise.
Dark is a fiction
cast by shadows
in our minds.

Eyes closed we see sparkles;
eyes open we see shadows,
always shadows.

I think of this now
in deep season
where snow brightens
my yard.

So shapes
show in even dark-night
rabbits and owls
moving about as shadows
upon my pearly earth.

They leave little sign
from daybreak on,
only small imprints:
wing hits, a blood drip here,
a four-footed hop, hop
nighttime feast
midnight deed.

Shadows
of what life has left
in its dark wake
of our passing
as we walk through
a winter sun west
and away.

SPRING

SOWING SEEDS - PART ONE

I'll trust the wind
and skies
to guide
a flower's way.

Were I the wind,
I would sow seeds early.
Float them to well watered spots,
filled with fertile soil,
where a sun ray might pierce
their tough outer husk,
wakening a sprout to struggle
toward the light,
ever rising
toward the light.

Wind, water,
sunshine, soil,
make a miracle in spring
with each new sprout
breaking ground,
greening, leafing
rising in just the right sun
in just the right shade
in just the right soil
with just enough water,
where it may thrive,
alive, climbing
for it to flower
for our pleasure.
What could be better?

Still,
I trust the wind
and skies
to guide a weed
or flower's way.

Sowing Seeds - part two

I sow seeds thick,
early in well-spaced,
well-watered rows
scarcely beneath soil,
where a sun ray may pierce
their tough outer husk,
wakening a sprout to struggle
toward the light.
Ever rising
toward the light.

They still grasp,
reaching down,
anchoring to the earth
with roots that follow
deep, deep deeper down,
as if gravity were
going to be not enough.

You can see a miracle
in each new sprout
breaking earth,
living in just the right sun
in just the right shade
in just the right soil
in just the very place
where it may thrive,
alive to bear fruit.

I sow my seeds wide,
not knowing
when I cast them,
which will survive

which might thrive.

For my eyes
are not so fine a guide
as the sky's breeze
that guides mother nature's
hands.

SWAN SONG

There is only so much to say
concerning the flight
of trumpeter swans,
sailing over this ice-filled
river on a bright spring
morning in March.

Words cannot match
what my eyes see,
here registered in memory
for future reference,
as the measure of a lithe
grand gesture.

The deep
wings stroke, driving across
a rising blue sky,
pure and sparkling
in a hush whir.

Hold onto this
I say,
hold tight this sight.
It clasps all meaning
of all life
ever created or conceived.

We must match that
beauty, bold, and striving,
to be ever
so fine.

SIGNS OF SPRING

This morning
well before light,
I hear a cardinal
singing up the sun,
high, high, higher perched,
atop a poplar tree out front.
Soon the tree standing by the drive
will leaf out.

The sun comes early,
now breaking southeast,
a little after coffee
sputters me awake
and I let the dogs out
to sniff the morning air
for rabbits and deer,
here where snow still holds.

Yesterday
two trumpeter swans
werc there in that open pool
across the river,
north where the ice opens early,
just a few yards wide.
First arrivers
can find a little food
from last season's growth,
heads ducking down
to fill their crops,
waiting more open water.

Today I see long shadows,
working through the morning woods.

Of all things in the universe,
nothing can be brighter
than this spring sun,
casting ever shifting shapes,
as I walk this sparkled,
snowy path.

Soon shadow and glow
will be dimmed down
as spring works warm magic
and the sun rises sky high.
Sap and leaves,
green sprouts,
pussy willow blooms,
pull eyes and mind
to summer things—
gardens, fish jumping,
frogs, and bugs galore.

But for now
just the river shore,
forest stark,
light and dark,
silent but for the crunch
of my foot fall.

Spring Morning

This morning
I am like the wind
spreading new life
on fresh spring soil.

But these lives were bought
in festive paper packets
at Ace hardware, downtown,
where new displays burst
with green garden promise,
and caught my eye,
as I stopped to imagine
summer's lush growth.

An odd mother nature
I am,
sore sitting here
on my garage floor
in small-town Minnesota,
where spring is more imaginary
than reality
through April.

I seed tomatoes, basil,
thyme, pansies, sage,
parsley and lavender.
Paper pots filled with new soil
are lined tight in trays.
Other seeds, bought in haste
will wait another day.

These pots I'll shelter,
all lined up marked in rows,

like school children waiting
to lift their heads,
raise their hands,
asking to take a turn
under the summer's sun.

If we are lucky
we will win this race
against nature.
A few early sprouts
will surge past spring
to bloom
under June's
warm sun.

MAY DAY

I have lived
wrapped in nature's arms
holding me tight
warm and nurtured.
It is as if I am a pupa
waiting to fly free
sensing that which
is out there
just beyond me.

I move always
taking note, making time,
searching a simple rhyme
for sounds outside myself
which sooth my soul.

And I wonder
why am I thrilled by thunder,
the dull thump of surf
striking a rocky shore,
or a roaring spring river
slipped over steep falls,
calling me, all calling me?

Or the murmur of frogs
at sunset in summer
rising from a pond's edge
just as the sun dips down,
or an owl in the night
hoot hooting just there
across the swamp?

I find no sounds better,
made by man or machine,
than those that pull me home,
than those I feel
walking the woods
at any time, in any season.

There is no time to stand still,
to rest or dream.
For me, I must just move on.

The crunch-pop of my footsteps
on moss or sticks,
the dry crumbling
or whoosh of set snow
is a carpet laid waiting
for my wander.

Spring Rain

I'll not walk
that river trail today.
Overnight rain
muddied the path
so it is sticky and slick.

I do not mind mud,
shoeless in summer
when a beaming sun
heats the shoreline
goo tickle-squishing
between my toes.

Today,
it could be warmer,
it could be drier,
it could be a sunny day.
A light breeze could be lilting
cardinal songs to me.

But no,
today's little drippy, cool rain
makes the grass grow,
greener by the drop.
Birch buds and pussy willows
begin to spread and pop.

All in all, given the wet,
it is perfect day,
for spring's certain yet.

ALL OF MY TIME

I did not sit to write
much this past week
due to fine weather
each day.
Flowers popping up
from bare soil unexpected
needed witnessing
to welcome them
back home.

Now that frost has lost
its war with the lilacs
and the tulips
have bloomed,
I must ready my acre
for beauty
and bounty.

All my time is taken:
seeds to sow
lawns to mow
boats to row
so May goes.

I wonder
will my gardens thrive
past drought
root rot
high wind
heat?

All of my time is taken,
so I did not sit to write

much this past week
due to fine weather.
I would rather greet
each sunrise
off and away
seeds to sow
lawns to mow
boats to row
on to June
I go.

SUMMER

FATHER'S DAY

Today marks small celebrations
of fathers good,
and fathers gone.
Simple recognition of their being,
as if a family could not be
without one rattling about
the basement
looking for his wrench.

They are like the rain that never fell
this June, when all the grasses dried.
I had to water and worry
waiting what finally fell today.
I welcome its coming,
as I would my father
come home from work late,
better than never.

Some mornings
coming home he hid
a chocolate bar in his lunch box,
under wrinkled waxed paper,
that mom used to carefully fold and wrap
his sandwiches the night before.
A surprise Hershey treat
vending machine bought
for the kids, he'd say,
and let us search and share,
as he passed through the kitchen.
kissed mom on the cheek,
and stumbled off to bed.
another midnight shift done.

So all fathers gift
their children life,
so mine gifted me
with generosity and a smile,
and my sisters
and my brothers.

There is nature and need
to all things meant to be
like rainfall and fathers.

WALKING THE MOUNTAIN'S EDGE

Sweat strained
flowers dripping past,
a kaleidoscope of blooms in June.
Purple bells, spangled pinks, tiny whites,
tripping at the knees
and ankle deep.
We stand to rest
before moving on
to see where it is
we have traveled
out of the rain forest.
From
as far as your eyes can see
to
as far as your eyes can see,
a bowl opens
rising off east a mile long.
Your eyes sweep over
ridge and peak
ridge and peak
faint glaciers sparkling
high off the island's core.
Bright rose red
flashing far off,
there!
higher than we will climb
higher than this path leads.

Out on the ridge line
here balanced precariously
on a thin trail drawn
in rock and mud across
the mountain's side,

a field perpendicular green
reaching cloud-blotched
down valley
west to ocean's edge.
Above, just south
sharp spires poke hard
dropping boulder spawn
here and there from the air
intersecting path and view
a gravity factory grey and hard.
North the ridge line rises
limey green-striped, steep-
slid with red volcanic muds
worked smooth here,
there green knobs.
Far below streams cut
rushing by huge spruce logs
falling down the mountain
unseen over the edge toward the sea,
pulsing through puffing lungs
on near mountain tops
the peaks great grey humps
higher higher still above,
and the sky turned ice
in morning's rising light
so deep blue.
From
as far as your eyes can see
to
as far as your eyes can see
you are transported.
A pretty piece of bursting color
moving quiet and slow
near the mountain's top
in June.

REFLECTION

In my life
every dawn was a new door.
Soft wind ruffled curtains
hung to hide morning's light,
but I greeted the breeze,
happy to see
another sun risen.
To hear again
that rust hinged screen door
rattle squeak,
looking out to see
past a gate across our drive
where a field danced
with sharp-tailed grouse
in midair,
like spirit birds,
above low morning fog,
formal and proud.
We too danced
the morning air.

In my life
storms cracked the sky
above that little pond
out back where cattails grew,
and we skated in winter,
roasting marshmallows,
over coals of a woodfire,
midnight on its shore,
cold night air
settling around us,
huddled, blowing away the flame,
waiting to cool the crust down.

In my life
we were never so cold
though the coals were dim,
never shivered.
Always my days were
filled with flowers,
bright spring blooms,
and pretty, kind ladies and gents
dressed in their summer best,
wearing those white cotton gloves,
veiled sun bonnets,
fedoras, jackets and ties.
You don't see that
much at all anymore;
all proper and elegant
at a time
when flowers and kindness
still persisted after the war.
They are still there
where I left them
just last night.

In my life
I have seen beauty
and touched love to my lips.
I have heard mourning doves
coo hoo, coo hoo at sunset.
All that matters
is the elegance,
the certainty, and respect.

Knowing all is well
for yet another day.
It is as if

I am a skipped stone
on calm waters.
The splash and rings
winding out across
a still, mirrored,
crystal universe.
l stand here
at a new door
waiting it to open.

Summer Rain

When I was a boy
and rain came to our cabin
in the night
I would hear a patter
on our thin plywood roof,
like the dance of toads or frogs
or lightning bugs.

I'd wonder
at its pit-a-pat drum
all the night long
melding my dreams
with dance and fun
a drum-a-drum-drum.

Come morning
out my lake window,
atop the higher bunk,
I'd see ducks
through dim morning light.
Little and big,
feather and fluff,
diving the weed beds,
making lily pads jump,
amongst bitty splish-splash
rain drops streaming
through our bay.

Slowly mist drifted over the lake
so quiet and calm
and I, a boy,
hoped to see sunshine
part the air,
a drum-a-drum-drum.

Morning Frost

My sleep ended early
this late summer day,
just after four,
before first-frost set
coating my squash vines.
A killing cover,
portending autumn
drifted down.

A cool crisp
mantle beyond
the firelight
flickering
in my hearth
and troubled heart.
All's silent but sputters
from the coffee machine
churning up my day,

It is a morose moment,
this early awakening,
dim and taut.
The last buds of my geraniums
dropped their petals in the night.
I feel their weight
as that of another
winter looming.

No, I cannot stop the season
no matter my wish or dream.
I cannot stop frost from forming.
Life is forever a steady progress,
edging each day

crossing the seasons
year by year by year.
I mull in the darkness
glacial aging calving bergs.

Nor can I take back
an insult once given,
or remove old, scarred wounds.
I cannot solve injustices I see
written in the morning news.
All are done deeds left better past
where summer lives.

My hope
is a new sunrise
showing all the bright
autumn colors hung,
the call of mourning doves
announcing a better day,
full harvest sparkling bright
the growing done.
I wait.

Peonies

Peonies are dancing
in the fog this morning
early
before the stunted dawn
a storm blown in
off the lake overnight.

Their long stems
bending pink, white,
peach blooms
bobbing beautiful
through waves of cool air
bright in the half light
of a new day.

Yesterday evening's heat
glowed from an over-hot sun
rising off these same blooms,
stifled. By end of day,
I prayed they would even survive
for the heat.

Isn't it amazing
how just one short night
can change all the expectations
of our future?

But now they chatter dance
happy wild alive
thriving
another day on the way!
Such is life.
Such is life.

Milkweed

June skies usually bring
enough sunny warm wet days
to keep the grass
green and lush,
but lacking rain this season
the lawn crackles brown,
crinkled and popping,
as I dance barefoot across
to the mailbox when I see
a small brown fur ball
sitting on the lawn.

I did not know
that rabbits eat milkweed
in times of drought.
It seems they will devour
anything even a little green.

I must weigh this
against monarch butterflies,
who usually visit
in July to feed
on my spreading milkweed,
thrive flitting around the yard,
where the bunny now
sits nibbling a milkweed stem,
his ears perked,
listening for me
to chase him away.

Should I leave the bunny
with his breakfast,
or save the butterfly's food?

Such choices are
hard to ponder over coffee,
waking to a warm summer sunrise.

I don't like playing god
early in the day.

Riverside

(Now I lay me down to sleep)

How was this riverside
left so rocky when
all 'round lie
soft rolling hills
of silt and sand?

(I pray the Lord my soul to keep)

What shrill force
thrust boulders aside
like dust, like feathers,
like leaves in the air
heaped now
in the jumble
I amble along
each day
on my way
through this calm woods
at riverside?

(And if I die before I wake)

Men have leveled
straight and true
the old railway line,
struck arrow-straight
though and though,
lying there across my river
slicing the shore
where locomotives
charge no more.

(I pray the lord my soul to take)

A berm built
to bleed this land dry:
all the prime timber cut,
all the fine fishes caught,
all the rich ores dug and gone,
hauled away south, north,
east and west,
the worthless rest
left to hobble my soul
on this rocky shore.

(If I should live for other days)

I dream
of having stood
before a waterfall,
where torrents stove great gouges
deep into the earth
tossed sidewise
flooding roars of mud
thrust off high
broken ice cliffs
calling me to stand back
where the land wore solid
below this icy end.

(I pray the Lord to guide my ways)

Here I rest,
a little warm,
wait the sun
where I live

between yesterday
and tomorrow.

Now I lay me
down to sleep.

Red-tailed Hawk

Look out there close!
See the red-tailed hawk scooting low
over those grasses
searching its prey?
Never forget that simple instant
he breaks his glide,
swoops down to ground,
up again, talons filled
on his way home.

Look to that forty acres
just north of the old McGregor track
there where once
old-growth white pine
towered high
then cut, hauled, burned over,
scoured clean for hay,
to feed the milkers
that kept a family alive
so many hard winters
ago.

Look to the top of the rise.
An old basement rests
dug deep
poured walls
not cheap,
left from a long gone
wood frame house
now burned,
abandoned.

All that's left
of someone's dream:
a home for a family,
build a barn,
grow some corn and oats,
feed the cattle and hens
take in some money
make a life.

All gone now.
All of life is change.

From trees to fields
to dreams and death
all a cycle
never ending
always starting
changing stopping
caught by the red-tailed hawk

Switched and gone
dug up, burned, buried.
The very topography
no longer rests where it was
but in our memory.

And when we die
we will fall in our forest
to become a tree
or fall in the field
and rise a flower
or fall in the river
and become a rock

Nothing is gained in death,
nor is anything lost.
We are all a piece
of the same cloth
waiting the Red-tailed hawk.

Oldenburg Point

Up on top of Oldenberg Point
where the CCC boys
built those old
stone shelters
we sat and gathered our wits to witness
seventy passed years.

Our lives
our ages resting
in this hulking grace
as if we were altogether
a part of a massive landmark
notched in the tree of time.

Each of us the limbs
off some whirling trunk
reaching out into the eons
with our eyes
and our dreams
and the dreams
of our sons and daughters
and the dreams
of their sons and daughters.

Here on Oldenburg Point
where the CCC boys
built paths and shelters and steps
to reach the river down.
We reached out to each other
and reveled in our time.

Now seeing each other for the first
or last time together,

a laughing and happy old bunch
with stories to tell.
So many tales.
Some true, many stretched,
but none forgotten
told here on Oldenburg Point.

Seventh Generation

We have seen this before
written on stone.
Words on papyrus.
Words on parchment.
Words on paper.
Words electric.
Words folded deep
in the creases of time,
lost, seeking redemption.

But only those sagas
written here by white pines,
their cursive roots winding,
across my path
through this dark grove,
will live to record,
an ancient knowing,
as they have always
told that tale.

These trees will speak,
snow laden bows,
white dusting the trail,
in winter season
when I am gone
still holding earth tight.

Their roots now roast
in dry ground
loosed all around,
heat riling their leaves,
bows bent,
as we muddle and fuss

turning the earth
overunderover
searching any wealth left
below an ever
more bare landscape.

The trees say,
"Let the earth rest!
Allow the winds to calm.
Leave us space
and time to renew.
We will do our work
to restore what you lay waste,
but slow."

Men have read
these signs before
written warnings on stone,
Words on papyrus.
Words on parchment.
Words on paper.
Words electric.

Words folded deep
in the creases of time
lost from the truth
spoken by trees:
saying
"Let the earth rest.
Let us breathe.
Let us hold the earth close."

What will we leave
to the seventh generation?

PLATE TECTONICS

Pressed,
our earth pulses
shimmer-sings
though every night,
screams sun beams
away each day,
hurtle spin-spinning
so quick
the light from our eyes
cannot catch its whirl.

I live this world,
whizzing fast
through cosmic voids
so quickly you'd think
simple friction
should have cooked
the meat from my bones
at the instant of my birth,
same every birth ever,
ever on.

But no!
I stand alive
past a half century
watching the skies
tumble past,
as I stumble along thinking,
"Life's a miracle."

My fortune is simple.
Winter's cold splits
the rough bark

of an old oak log,
just as my own life
has torn
as it ages
and breaks.

But we are each forever,
the oak and I.
Seasoned and spun.
Seasoned and spun.
Turned to ashes, dust,
buried deep into
this earth's crust
then risen,
ever risen anew.

Waiting Autumn

I see the photo:
an old man
holding a huge trout,
smiling broadly
above his own
morning edition
obituary.

Already anticipation
has eaten a hole
in the morning sky.
There,
under the streetlight,
a shadow passes
carrying memories
of other waiting days:
A late night phone call
that never came,
or that sunny afternoon
the mailman might
bring me words-
just one letter please-
of love.

So I wait for this fog to lift
sun to rise up.
I can start fresh
under blue sky.

Last week
maple, oak, ash
red, green, yellow
bursts drifted down

as I walked woodland trails
through their paisley carpet,
my eyes struck by
beautiful shades
against the backdrop
buck bush and mosses
of greens so green.

A world without match
I thought,
until yesterday when again
I strolled
looking to see
changes brought by
shorter days
cooling nights.

Then came the birches.
all the birches
standing tall now,
young straining up
sparkling white-bared branches
in sunlit roadside groves
so near stark
on fern browned ground
against the bluest deep sky.

I am keen
to see what next week
brings to me.

I see the photo
of an old man
smiling bright
holding a huge trout,

above his own obituary
morning paper
waiting.

River Walk

I can tell you now,
honestly,
my bones are tired,
and I am lost.

The moon's glow
haunts me here this eve
where all the night's a mirror
of my shadowed past.
I wonder
from where do we spring?

What vision calls us to be?
Some dim reflection,
or a sweet odor rising in the night
as we walk the river path,
talk to water's shimmer,
tell it our stories
riding its ripple south.

What force rises us
like sap in spring trees?
Here, there
winter away,
spring risen again,
summer sun warming,
ever on.

How does mother earth
assign our return?
We have no leaves
no pretty petals
no bursting fruit

to please her eyes
full, ripe, new life.

Will I be a loon's warble?
You a bullfrog's harrumph?
Or will we be the simple rustle
of leaves at autumn's fall
stepping down to winter rest
as we reach the other side?

I only know now,
from where I stand
there is no end,
but beginnings
beginning again.

SUDDENLY

I've become my father
old and gray
standing at the sink
with that five-mile-
morning stare looking
out the alcove window
watching for the sun.

Morning coffee cooling
my mind,
trying to collect,
connect,
last night's muddled dreams,
with that fine potato
I grew
and dug last evening
just as the sun dropped,
lying on the counter top
washed and ready.

That is all that is left
of a long life
well lived
now standing
by the kitchen sink
waiting another day.

Forest

This morning
as the sun rises
hot and dry,
my footsteps
crunch leaves
drifted down in the night,
so still and dense
a near stream
ripples by unheard.

I think
there is more god
in a grain of sand
or gnarled old oak,
than any cathedral,
church, temple, or mosque
ever built by man.

Here where the water
flows free
the forest floor
carries a rhythm never imagined.
We are insignificant.
We are of this world.
We are as grains of sand,
or leaves on a tree,
set adrift in life
unleashed.
We are set free.

I will do my worshiping here
inside all creation
where wind and water

wears earth to sand
and bears it down
to rest and rise
rest and rise.

For there is more god
in a grain of sand
or gnarled old oak,
than any cathedral,
church, temple, or mosque
ever built to hold
a god made by man.

CARRY THE STORY FORWARD

I'm beginning to see
little splashes of color
here and there off in the tree-
tops, stopping to look
at goldens and reds
popping through green
summer leaves.

Little autumn lights splash,
born of cool nights
forcing summer's sweet syrups
to turn and run back,
return to the roots
to rest for season.

Time turns here
in this hardwood-softwood-
mixed wood, old
sugar maple forest.

Where the sun's early rise in March
drives sleeping cells awake
to churn, suck,
pull and pump
those silent nectars from deep,
up through the trunk
to fat limbs
coursing sprouted buds
who burst limey open in May,
grow dark green in June,
and flourish rustling through July.

Now drained,

the juice done,
veins dried,
sun stoked, wind-blown-down
to burst on my world
red gold rust
but opening the
bluest-blue sky to me
even before the first snow flies.

What could possibly
be better than that?

AUTUMN

CAROUSEL

Autumn is a colorful carousel
each leaf-life
spinning off to
a future fate
designed
to make the world
more bright
in another turn of the sun.

I feel a lurking sadness
to summer's end
filtered through the splendor
of bursting autumn reds
yellows bronze gold
flashing sunrise.

Each leaf transforms.
Blows loose, floats
to huddle down
with the mushrooms
now bursting
all along my woodland path.

These pretty, bright
falling leaves,
dropped to ground,
at just the right time
for mushrooms to
consume them
from what has been left
of all that would
elsewise die
including you and I.

Autumn is a colorful carousel.
Each leaf-life
spinning off to
a future fate
designed
to make the world
more bright
in another turn of the sun.

September

Here lies the harvest
fast piled, rough
with all we can stuff
our chipmunk cheeks
puffed and bulging,
or squirrels or ants
or bees with their combs.

I relish the ripeness
of September
just after the rot sets in
when last apples drop,
deer come at night
to feast on our fallen bounty.
Leaf edges brown here, then there,
the maples, sweet and red,
drip to the ground
drowned in morning dew.

At evening I see
a thousand varied birds
fowl big, fowl small
flocking south-
go south, go south
they shout, stroking
the air
seeking fresh wheat berries
and grasses still green,
as frost turns my world white.

We fight the famine
as if our fate rests
still in those ancient caves

with bright open blazes
where only our hands
or faces and feet warmed
so we hold
so we hold
fearing night, fearing cold.

For me?
I wait the rest of winter.
I wait the Northern lights.
I wait to touch the stars
and hear an icy crackle
as I step off the porch
into the night.

September's End

The forest floor grows
deep with leaves
falling fast now
in autumn's last heat.
Snipe and woodcock,
long-beaked, hungry
browse through
thrash the litter
tossing, turning, searching
a succulent bug
to fill their bellies
before heading south
with most other
intelligent fowl.

Aged rotting stumps
set the forest 'round,
draped in mushrooms and moss
tell tales of a towering past.
Where oaks still stand tall,
grassy ground beneath
beaded with acorn caps,
red squirrels, grouse,
deer, bear,
all feast in autumn's
fat fall.

The forest is still
thick with green
understory—
raspberry, alder,
sumac, nettles
milkweed, cattails,

swamp grass, more,
all ripe or wilting
back to their damp beginnings,
oozing their lives into the earth
for next spring's sprouts.

FOREST FLOOR

I ask you,
walk with me,
brighten my autumn afternoon,
with your swirling colors
this shiny bright day,
limbs wavering above
gusting breeze, stealing
those leafy summer burdens,
dance-whirling
through clear blue skies,
to clutter this narrow path
through my forest
lime, yellow, orange, red
all spun free
a carpet for this new season.

It is as if every year,
each tree's dreams drift
to fade under my feet,
where once they hung
so expectant,
lush green,
high and deep,
anticipations of summer sun
now dry blown
by season's swing
fallen, but never gone
coating my path
my forest floor
with a lovely autumn luster
dreams lost
new visions beckon.

Ruffed Grouse

Three am
sky's clear
each star a bright blinking beacon,
even where the earth's
horizon hides.

Four am
mist fog flows down
east off Lake Superior,
driven by an unseen sun rising
there where the earth begins.

My valley still
awaits the beginning
of the end of new beginnings.
Trees weep leaves
falling clear,
golden brown red rust,
limbs finally relieved
of summer's burden
joyful sun streams through.

Grouse are about
in mid-September
as first frosts chill the air
in bubbles and pockets
alder thickets and bogs.
I wait that signaling drum
burst out of tall grass
along the trail side
grouse aloft gone.
Quicker than quick!
finger near the trigger

and safety ready
I fire a miss.

I always carry
extra shotgun shells
in a burlap side bag
strung on a leather strap
hung off my shoulder
so as not to
interfere with pulling
shotgun up to aim, shoot
which I do often,
but don't hit many
hunting grouse
each autumn.

HUNTING HOUNDS

Soon,
after we get a little light
I will pack up the pups,
head out for a long walk
through the woods.
Calm.

As daylight breaks
We taste a new forest.
They, the mosses and rocks,
me, cool spruce.
Sumac's seductive musk,
will pocket the air,
here and there.

When sun is up
we will gaze
through an open,
stark woodland,
bare but busy,
shadow and light.
So, we wait.
Calm.

Now
the leaves are fallen,
earth damp with their rot.
Sound rides far and fast
cutting quick
each click of a branch
broken ten yards off,
as a rabbit jumps just there.
The pups dash

pulling their long leads,
ears perked high
wanting to chase
where the bunny bursts.

I do not shoot rabbits,
but did once when young.
Never again.
They cry if they are hurt.
I have no heart for tears
anymore.

OCTOBER

Don't be an old fool
my dear,
the willows are not all dying.
It is clear. The skies
will be more blue
the ground white and bright
just after the sunrise
all the winter long
with willow leaves fallen,
gone.

Don't fret the loss.
Forever it is not.
Chittering flocks of redwings
will trill next spring,
if not now,
as cold closes,
your bright world dims,
with early sunset days,
another season down.

Don't believe
those now fallen leaves
will not rise again
sap flowing next spring.
It is always, ever true
that one season
is a beginning
of the next
never an end
does never end.
It can never end.
Life never ends.

Don't worry
your silly self
over the early snow
dropped on the lawn
where lives still green
down underneath.
There the voles
and wiggly worms
winter through
just as you,
to spring.

ALL SAINTS' EVE

Short days ahead
long, longer nights
dreams filled
with lives
I did not lead
paths I did not follow,
corners not turned.
So many adventures
just off the horizon
where they will always be waiting
some other summer day.

I do not want autumn
to ever end.
Its fallen leaves cover
in mists of a life lived
with bright shades
all oranges reds
beautiful beds
filled with possibility.

Soon gossamer frost
will crystal morning earth,
sparkling across the lawn's
moonlit night.
At dawn there'll be
frost-fine footprints
another summer gone.

In dreams
I've lived lives
I never knew,
shadow boxes filled

with people, places
ignored forgotten
seen not noted
flashing past
like cards shuffled
deck not dealt.

My past dreams
mysteries
closed,
I do not want autumn
to ever end.

HUNTING WITH BOB ROSS

I was watching Bob Ross
make the sky, brush-a-brush
dark, darker blue blended
light, lighter, so light down,
'til it reached blue white water
soon darker blue, dark water.

As Bob Ross melded his portrait world
all frizzy haired and skinny,
his easel filled with stories
of painting the earth,
making his world soft and smooth,
soft and smooth
enough to make me dream.

Hunting is all about the story
my palette about the game,
or a triumphant hunt,
or outwitting the witless,
or seeing that huge old track,
or the covey that flew too fast,
or a valley so brimming with,
joy, I could not shoot.
I could not pull the trigger.

So I walk, listen,
look and look
see and hear
seeking a light little crack
off in the murky brush.
Those tight thick spots
where a grouse might huddle up
or strut slowly off

as I walk away
seeking a story
to take home to tell
again and again.

A blank canvas of my world
from my eyes to yours
my ears to yours
all the sounds of whispering
howling, creaking trees,
the smell of ripe sumac
dusky cedar sharp,
pressing in around my trail,
dark blue, light,
and more light
as we walk
a drifting trail,
toward the lake.

Hunting Zen

So still, quiet.
It feels as if death looms near
even on this sunny morn.
Standing here high
in clear winter cold
hung above buck brush
in an icy metal tree stand,
I feel the freeze
deep pulling me down.

Then off to the west
in the dark bog ahead I hear
a snap pierce dark shadows.

I turn
peak my old ears
to hear another
then a thud
and the swish of dried grasses
so still the sun
warming my back
shadow crisp
cold still
no deer
mystery.

The swoosh
of raven's wings
floats high above
the bare poplars
where I tensely sit
and wait and wait and wait
only to see

chickadee-dee-dee,
hear a downy woodpecker
climbing an old dead tree
and fifty yards off swamp side
the rustle of a red squirrel
setting off on his day.

But not a step,
no walk-trot
coming fast through those
hummocks and spruce ahead,
just hushed silence
enclosing
me
the tree
cold breeze
the sun
we are one.

Big as a Mountain

An autumn chill
has followed
the wind down
around my home
here by the river.
Low bushes, sumac
washed yellow red brown
speckle the hedge row
so green.
I have seen,
this summer
now long, autumn
has begun.

My life's
been paced by these
simple transitions:
spring, summer, fall, winter
morning, noon, evening, night
second, minute, hour, day.
day, week, month, year
all counts tracking
a mind filled with dreams
as big as mountains.

So still they rise
at this late date,
unannounced,
looming large as Everest
popping up through the mist.
I wonder
at the splendor
of this new season

imagining a path
through the clouds
to tippy top sky
as the leaves turn their faces
down to fall brown
calling winter's
ice covered snow.

As a child I imagined
I was prince
of a stuffed toy kingdom
napping upstairs afternoons,
hush whispering to Teddy,
telling him my tales.
We were explorers,
warriors valiant.

He saved me
and I him
in our heroic world
rescuing damsels,
gaining gold and pearls,
as we listened for mother's voice
calling from downstairs
to milk and cookies
one for all and
all for one.

So simple fantasy
taught friendship, trust
and belief that there was good
to be found just beyond.
a string of dreams
heroic ambitions.
Love conquering all,

leading me here now,
to this autumn year
near seventy years passed.

Still these dreams
carry me forward
year after year
as I wait my mother's voice
calling me down
for milk and cookies
as winter comes on.

Cabin

You would think
this forest empty
if you crept quiet
through the
musty damp-leaved
carpet.

Bare oaks, maple,
ash, stick stark,
high against a gray sky,
others lie along
the ground tipped,
felled, fallen
some from winds
in winters long past.

They huddle warm
beneath the leaves
peeking lichen
mosses green
ground pine poking.

These old trees feed
the winter forest floor
leading us to
our next life
and the next
through cold dark winters.

Snow will soon drape them
like an abandoned cabin—
dust cloth covered couches—
awaiting spring

and the children running
singing cheery,
bright songs.

East Northeast

My land is a cold, old land
growing maple, oak
birch, and poplar
to fill a void once held by others.
Bright frost-bit leaves
and bared branches,
won't hold fall winds
from chilling my bones.

East northeast breezes
blowing low off
Otchipwe-kitchi-gami
flow down to me here
on the Kettle River drainage.
Cold mists rise off
warmed summer lake waters.

Here, now,
winds cut far further south
than when the great old growth
pine forests stood.
My father's father,
and his brothers, too,
cut all the forest down,
slashed what lay left
of a millennium.

Autumn's winds were held high
by great white and red pine,
huge spruce and cedar walls,
where winds flew past,
wild rice ripened, warmed,
red winged black birds

ducks, swans and geese
flocked to feast, safe
for their long flight south.

Trees tall, green forever,
towering triumphant old growth,
held the land in place,
kept trout and sturgeon fed,
moose and elk sheltered,
held the people safe
warm from winter's cold.

No more.
My father's father,
and his brothers, too,
cut all the forest down,
slashed what lay left,
and burned the rest
gone.

My land is a cold old land
filled with maple, oak,
birch and poplar,
pretty to see,
but no match
for the late lake winds,
to keep cold from my bones.

LOGGED LAND

Along this old logging trail
still all the bushes are dense
leafy green
so I hunt with Sadie's ears
pointed left right left ahead
as she perks and peaks
with every crick and peep
I cannot hear.

Each autumn a surprise to see
old forest cut to ground, gone.
Or last year's new rising,
popping head high already
tight with poplar sprout.
The ground transformed
twisted, torn reborn,
season after season after season.

I will tell you
when I was a boy these very acres
were abandoned farmers' fields
cleared in hand-grubbed rock piles
horse pulled roots. Then
emptied with the Depression
when everything went bust.
Everything went bust;
all the old people left.

Still there grow aged apple trees
and plums
draped at the edge
of a caved root cellar
and the foundation ring,

a family farmhouse,
twisted and ripped by roots
now sixty years passed.
Logged once already,
ready for logging again.
Dust to dust
to dust
to dust.

Tomorrow
I will show you
a new spot to walk
with Sam and Sadie
my ever-eager canine friends.
A new trail
where the way is not clear
where each new curve, stop,
rise, drop, creek, or hill
will offer views fresh and new
to their senses
lesser mine.

I am not
done seeing forests grow—
watching sweet summers pass
through autumn to winter,
hearing the leaves rustle as they fall
deep and deeper,
swishing along our routes.

There are always new paths to wander
out here in the woods
where grouse drum spring and fall.
There is no place where
the earth does not grow

and change
grow and change.
It pleases my eyes
and the pup's noses
as they scent a bird
running wild ahead,
always
the birds running
wild ahead
drawing us on.

First Snow

Early morning
flakes falling
late this season
Just short an inch
brightening a moonless dark
first of December,
four a.m.

I awoke
from a deep dream
remembering
I did not finish my
yard work yesterday
as it grew late
and I was tired of raking,
pulling dead stuff off the ground,
putting summer tools away.
Now those have no matter
for summer past
is covered over finally,
hidden under a new drape,
fresh gone.

My life measured
by seasonal switches
Easter baskets
May flowers
memorial flags
Fourth-of-July bangs
through turkey
past Christmas
to a new year
winding away,

a parade
each year I have
lived on this earth.

The days are like
these sparkling flakes
drifting past as I wander
a cool morning cluttered
with the memories
slowly shushing under,
here a new,
there an old,
collecting on the path,
wind-whipped
white whirling,
piling by my boots.

As a kid I
imagined the sound
sugar plum fairies
might make,
never knowing where
or what they might be,
suspecting sparkly bright
red-dressed elves
dancing fanciful music
of bells.

Now I know
it is the sound of snow,
the quiet peace
bringing winter,
a world more light,
more sweet and lively
finally again begun.

Northern Lights

The northern lights
announced themselves
just last night,:
a chorus of colors flowing
glorious, prismatic, bright,
shadowed rhythms,
thrusting between
earth and sky.

All the while
I slept deeply,
neither song nor dance
did waken me,
dreaming instead
of leaves falling
all red, amber, and brown
and the whisper
of winter coming on.

I wish I had woken
to see the sky dancing,
lights refracting,
spinning shades
telling tales
giving guidance
and beauty on
this first cool
autumn night.

Such sights
make minds weave stories
told over eons,
sitting before glowing coals,

to look up to see
how the sky
talks to big bear,
little dipper,
drawing new truths,
pulsing music and color,
weaving the night
in the dance of time.

EPILOGUE

Old Growth

Part One

Follow me away
this four lane road rush
trucks tires whir bump
drumming asphalt
thrumming past
an incessant hum
like water over a fall
push prod pulsing
gaining faster
where
there
is
no sweet grotto,
no silence,
no end.

Don't you see
we cannot keep
up this pace?
Pull over
by that dirt lane.
Stop.

I know a path
leading west
toward day's end,
where a winding track
drops down a valley
to a quiet haven
a narrow brook

still trout linger
under grassy banks,
willows hanging
low below here
the world quiet.
We will watch water
slowly pool
and flow
toward
great
rivers
simple progress
like thoughts we forgot
in our rush.

This world
was well settled
before our convictions
ripped roots loose
built roads, bridges,
levies, dams.
Stole every accessible inch
of worth from the soil
the very marrow earth's bones
sucked dry dug torn
refined filled replaced.
If it was green
we cut all of it
down.

OLD GROWTH

PART TWO

I think
the world is burning
and we are inside.
Walking in autumn
I rustle leaves piled high
my path made
and lost buried under, fallen
step by step
with one small
puff of sky
dry, so dry,
we are lost.

Most don't go much
into real woods anymore,
where only animal paths
wind through dense
swamp, bog,
ridge, and valley.
Paths wind
along stream banks
up steep slopes
around about forests.
Easy to lose
wander off lost
if you don't watch
your way.
Most would rather follow
man-made paths,
old logging roads,

abandoned rail lines,
left after all the good logs
were cut, graded, sawn.
Prime ore dug,
shipped, smelted
gone.

The sweet scent
of a verdant past
grows beside
these remnant lanes,
earth's scarred marks,
made by my father, your father,
and their father's before them.
We look back to see
these trails our ancestors
built and abandoned
now roads to nowhere
from nowhere.
All the value gone.

Old Growth

Part Three

Let me take you
into the trees
there where every
story ever told
lies within stands
so stately
as if orations.
They speak our roots,
visions, hopes, dreams
all enclosed
within a green canopy.

Here you will
feel the moss
under your feet,
sniff the wet wind,
smell all of life
fecund ripe,
a birthing mother.

In summer
each tree
filling a wood
whistle-sings, wind
whispers dawns
flutters days
through to sunset
darkest night
where owls
perch high
and wait.

Birch, black oak,
poplar, pine, ash,
maple, oak, elm,
basswood, fir,
talking different dialects,
taught by wind and rain
greeting new each day.
Each season
a new chatter
reflecting sun or frost,
heat or rain,
breeze or blow,
tipping shifting,
their limbs wobble-wave
a Gregorian hum
announcing, "I am here.
We are here.
We the forest."

Old Growth

Part Four

In this still
hot August
midday steaming
fern forest glade
sounds creak crick snap
whoosh.
We walk
pushing aside
buck brush,
hazel nut,
stumbling ruts,
and deadfalls
surveying a little piece
of earth
to find a small spot
swamp side,
a mossy stump
where grasses
divide damp dirt
from soggy
under mud.

Long-lain tipped over
trunks taken
decades past
by wind or rot
lie fallen
like you or I
might fall
someday but not

today.
We rest sweat
here where they lie.

One toppled poplar,
moss-humped,
laced with brown-black
mushroom cups
standing off the gray rotted bark
stretches east a hundred feet
settled deep
busy being
new forest food.

It looks to have been
stately in its time.
We have no obituary
recording its life.
Still, it lies
feeding the forest
nurturing progeny
as we rest our eyes.

It is so quiet
we can hear
a leaf's fall.
We are at rest
seeing the forest,
just watching
shadows move through
the trees.

When I die
I dream to lie beneath
this canopy,

cleaved open to the sun,
a stream of rays
driven past leaves
slicing green shadows
through damp air
beaming me still
in this sweet rot.

Surely violets
will spring next season,
or a tiny toad haven
will find a crevasse,
where once roots grew.
Perhaps a rabbit
will nest its young
in the shade
of the fallen.
So we will
all enter earth,
all the while
lives moving on.

And when I die
I will lie
beside them.
Even the finest
old tree topples,
lies silent,
standing tall
only a memory
becoming reborn
to old growth.

About the Author

Patrick Stevens is a life long teacher, nature lover, and writer. Upon graduation from the University of Minnesota in 1974, Stevens taught high school English in Grygla, Minnesota.

In 1977 he migrated to Sitka, Alaska where he taught middle school language arts for twenty years. Retiring in 1997, he became an instructor for the University of Alaska, Southeast until relocating to Moose Lake, Minnesota in 2002. There he worked in the education department for the Minnesota Department of Corrections as a librarian and educational supervisor. He fully retired in the spring of 2008.

The book *Natural Wonders* is a collection of poems about experiencing the northern forest in all seasons of the year. Stevens says, "Hiking, hunting, observing, gardening and simply investing time in the woods is all that matters. Truly."

Acknowledgments

Without the help of Kathleen Stamm and Kath O'Keefe this book would have never come to print. They devoted time to a project that has little benefit to them. I thank them both for all of their hand holding, encouragement, time, and editing in making the collection a reality.

Noteworthy, too, are my graphic designer, Carol Squicci, and my publishing advisor, Tim Jollymore.

FINNS WAY BOOKS

The advent of *Natural Wonders*, culled from a much larger body of Mr. Stevens's work, is quite in keeping with the advocacy of Finns Way Books which is to annually publish a small number of books of poetry and fiction which cast the individual in natural settings, beset by phenomenon of the physical world outdoors and by the interior struggles of his or her own psyche.

In that endeavor, the work of Patrick Stevens is a welcomed and pithy addition.

Walter Lumppio,
General Principal,
Finns Way Books

www.ingramcontent.com/pod-product-compliance
Lightning Source LLC
Chambersburg PA
CBHW032058020426
42335CB00011B/389

* 9 7 9 8 9 8 9 9 9 4 2 2 0 6 *